MW01234052

DAILY SOBRIETY RECOVERY JOURNAL

Days Sober □

Date :_____ S M T W R F S

Any Triggers today? Yes No

Appetite _____

Exercise today _____

Water Intake

8 oz	8 oz	8 oz	8 oz	8 oz	8 oz	8 oz	8 oz
8 oz	8 oz	8 oz	8 oz	8 oz	8 oz	8 oz	8 oz

Hour Slept 1 2 3 4 5 6 7 8 9 10 11 12

Anxiety Level Today 1 2 3 4 5 6 7 8 9 10

Sadness Level Today 1 2 3 4 5 6 7 8 9 10

Cravings Level Today 1 2 3 4 5 6 7 8 9 10

Daily Reflection

Goal for today...

_____

_____

_____

I am proud of...

_____

_____

_____

I'm grateful for...

_____

_____

_____

Positive affirmation ...

_____

_____

_____

Days Sober ☐

Date :_____ S M T W R F S

Any Triggers today? Yes No

Appetite _____

Exercise today _____

Water Intake

8 oz	8 oz	8 oz	8 oz	8 oz	8 oz	8 oz	8 oz
8 oz	8 oz	8 oz	8 oz	8 oz	8 oz	8 oz	8 oz

Hour Slept 1 2 3 4 5 6 7 8 9 10 11 12

Anxiety Level Today 1 2 3 4 5 6 7 8 9 10

Sadness Level Today 1 2 3 4 5 6 7 8 9 10

Cravings Level Today 1 2 3 4 5 6 7 8 9 10

Daily Reflection

Goal for today...

_____

_____

_____

I am proud of...

_____

_____

_____

I´m grateful for...

_____

_____

_____

Positive affirmation ...

_____

_____

_____

Days Sober □

Date : _____ S M T W R F S

Any Triggers today? Yes No

Appetite _____

Exercise today _____

Water Intake

8 oz	8 oz	8 oz	8 oz	8 oz	8 oz	8 oz	8 oz
8 oz	8 oz	8 oz	8 oz	8 oz	8 oz	8 oz	8 oz

Hour Slept 1 2 3 4 5 6 7 8 9 10 11 12

Anxiety Level Today 1 2 3 4 5 6 7 8 9 10

Sadness Level Today 1 2 3 4 5 6 7 8 9 10

Cravings Level Today 1 2 3 4 5 6 7 8 9 10

Daily Reflection

Goal for today...

_____

_____

_____

I am proud of...

_____

_____

_____

I´m grateful for...

_____

_____

_____

Positive affirmation ...

_____

_____

_____

Days Sober ☐

Date :＿＿＿＿＿＿ S M T W R F S

Any Triggers today? Yes No

Appetite ＿＿＿＿＿＿＿＿＿＿＿＿＿＿＿＿＿＿＿＿＿

Exercise today ＿＿＿＿＿＿＿＿＿＿＿＿＿＿＿＿＿

Water Intake

8 oz	8 oz	8 oz	8 oz	8 oz	8 oz	8 oz	8 oz
8 oz	8 oz	8 oz	8 oz	8 oz	8 oz	8 oz	8 oz

Hour Slept 1 2 3 4 5 6 7 8 9 10 11 12

Anxiety Level Today 1 2 3 4 5 6 7 8 9 10

Sadness Level Today 1 2 3 4 5 6 7 8 9 10

Cravings Level Today 1 2 3 4 5 6 7 8 9 10

Daily Reflection

Goal for today...

_____

_____

_____

I am proud of...

_____

_____

_____

I'm grateful for...

_____

_____

_____

Positive affirmation ...

_____

_____

_____

Days Sober ☐

Date :_____ S M T W R F S

Any Triggers today? Yes No

Appetite _____

Exercise today _____

Water Intake

8 oz	8 oz	8 oz	8 oz	8 oz	8 oz	8 oz	8 oz
8 oz	8 oz	8 oz	8 oz	8 oz	8 oz	8 oz	8 oz

Hour Slept 1 2 3 4 5 6 7 8 9 10 11 12

Anxiety Level Today 1 2 3 4 5 6 7 8 9 10

Sadness Level Today 1 2 3 4 5 6 7 8 9 10

Cravings Level Today 1 2 3 4 5 6 7 8 9 10

Daily Reflection

Goal for today...

_____

_____

_____

I am proud of...

_____

_____

_____

I′m grateful for...

_____

_____

_____

Positive affirmation ...

_____

_____

_____

Days Sober ☐

Date :_____ S M T W R F S

Any Triggers today? Yes No

Appetite _____

Exercise today _____

Water Intake

8 oz	8 oz	8 oz	8 oz	8 oz	8 oz	8 oz	8 oz
8 oz	8 oz	8 oz	8 oz	8 oz	8 oz	8 oz	8 oz

Hour Slept 1 2 3 4 5 6 7 8 9 10 11 12

Anxiety Level Today 1 2 3 4 5 6 7 8 9 10

Sadness Level Today 1 2 3 4 5 6 7 8 9 10

Cravings Level Today 1 2 3 4 5 6 7 8 9 10

Daily Reflection

Goal for today...

_____

_____

_____

I am proud of...

_____

_____

_____

I'm grateful for...

_____

_____

_____

Positive affirmation ...

_____

_____

_____

Days Sober ☐

Date :_____ S M T W R F S

Any Triggers today? Yes No

Appetite _____

Exercise today _____

Water Intake

8 oz	8 oz	8 oz	8 oz	8 oz	8 oz	8 oz	8 oz
8 oz	8 oz	8 oz	8 oz	8 oz	8 oz	8 oz	8 oz

Hour Slept 1 2 3 4 5 6 7 8 9 10 11 12

Anxiety Level Today 1 2 3 4 5 6 7 8 9 10

Sadness Level Today 1 2 3 4 5 6 7 8 9 10

Cravings Level Today 1 2 3 4 5 6 7 8 9 10

Daily Reflection

Goal for today...

_____

_____

_____

I am proud of...

_____

_____

_____

I´m grateful for...

_____

_____

_____

Positive affirmation ...

_____

_____

_____

Days Sober ☐

Date : _____ S M T W R F S

Any Triggers today? Yes No

Appetite _____

Exercise today _____

Water Intake

8 oz	8 oz	8 oz	8 oz	8 oz	8 oz	8 oz	8 oz
8 oz	8 oz	8 oz	8 oz	8 oz	8 oz	8 oz	8 oz

Hour Slept 1 2 3 4 5 6 7 8 9 10 11 12

Anxiety Level Today 1 2 3 4 5 6 7 8 9 10

Sadness Level Today 1 2 3 4 5 6 7 8 9 10

Cravings Level Today 1 2 3 4 5 6 7 8 9 10

Daily Reflection

Goal for today...

_____

_____

_____

I am proud of...

_____

_____

_____

I'm grateful for...

_____

_____

_____

Positive affirmation ...

_____

_____

_____

Days Sober ☐

Date : _____ S M T W R F S

Any Triggers today? Yes No

Appetite _____

Exercise today _____

Water Intake

8 oz	8 oz	8 oz	8 oz	8 oz	8 oz	8 oz	8 oz
8 oz	8 oz	8 oz	8 oz	8 oz	8 oz	8 oz	8 oz

Hour Slept 1 2 3 4 5 6 7 8 9 10 11 12

Anxiety Level Today 1 2 3 4 5 6 7 8 9 10

Sadness Level Today 1 2 3 4 5 6 7 8 9 10

Cravings Level Today 1 2 3 4 5 6 7 8 9 10

Daily Reflection

Goal for today...

_____

_____

_____

I am proud of...

_____

_____

I'm grateful for...

_____

_____

Positive affirmation ...

_____

_____

Days Sober ☐

Date :_____ S M T W R F S

Any Triggers today? Yes No

Appetite _____

Exercise today _____

Water Intake | 8 oz | 8 oz | 8 oz | 8 oz | 8 oz | 8 oz | 8 oz | 8 oz |
| 8 oz | 8 oz | 8 oz | 8 oz | 8 oz | 8 oz | 8 oz | 8 oz |

Hour Slept 1 2 3 4 5 6 7 8 9 10 11 12

Anxiety Level Today 1 2 3 4 5 6 7 8 9 10

Sadness Level Today 1 2 3 4 5 6 7 8 9 10

Cravings Level Today 1 2 3 4 5 6 7 8 9 10

Daily Reflection

Goal for today...

_____

_____

_____

I am proud of...

_____

_____

_____

I´m grateful for...

_____

_____

_____

Positive affirmation ...

_____

_____

_____

Days Sober ☐

Date :_____ S M T W R F S

Any Triggers today? Yes No

Appetite _____

Exercise today _____

Water Intake

8 oz	8 oz	8 oz	8 oz	8 oz	8 oz	8 oz	8 oz
8 oz	8 oz	8 oz	8 oz	8 oz	8 oz	8 oz	8 oz

Hour Slept 1 2 3 4 5 6 7 8 9 10 11 12

Anxiety Level Today 1 2 3 4 5 6 7 8 9 10

Sadness Level Today 1 2 3 4 5 6 7 8 9 10

Cravings Level Today 1 2 3 4 5 6 7 8 9 10

Daily Reflection

Goal for today...

_____

_____

_____

I am proud of...

_____

_____

_____

I´m grateful for...

_____

_____

_____

Positive affirmation ...

_____

_____

_____

Days Sober ☐

Date :_____ S M T W R F S

Any Triggers today? Yes No

Appetite _____

Exercise today _____

Water Intake

8 oz	8 oz	8 oz	8 oz	8 oz	8 oz	8 oz	8 oz
8 oz	8 oz	8 oz	8 oz	8 oz	8 oz	8 oz	8 oz

Hour Slept 1 2 3 4 5 6 7 8 9 10 11 12

Anxiety Level Today 1 2 3 4 5 6 7 8 9 10

Sadness Level Today 1 2 3 4 5 6 7 8 9 10

Cravings Level Today 1 2 3 4 5 6 7 8 9 10

Daily Reflection

Goal for today...

_____

_____

_____

I am proud of...

_____

_____

I ' m grateful for...

_____

_____

Positive affirmation ...

_____

_____

Days Sober ☐

Date : _____ S M T W R F S

Any Triggers today? Yes No

Appetite _____

Exercise today _____

Water Intake

8 oz	8 oz	8 oz	8 oz	8 oz	8 oz	8 oz	8 oz
8 oz	8 oz	8 oz	8 oz	8 oz	8 oz	8 oz	8 oz

Hour Slept 1 2 3 4 5 6 7 8 9 10 11 12

Anxiety Level Today 1 2 3 4 5 6 7 8 9 10

Sadness Level Today 1 2 3 4 5 6 7 8 9 10

Cravings Level Today 1 2 3 4 5 6 7 8 9 10

Daily Reflection

Goal for today...

_____

_____

_____

I am proud of...

_____

_____

_____

I'm grateful for...

_____

_____

_____

Positive affirmation ...

_____

_____

_____

Days Sober ☐

Date :_____ S M T W R F S

Any Triggers today? Yes No

Appetite _____

Exercise today _____

Water Intake

8 oz	8 oz	8 oz	8 oz	8 oz	8 oz	8 oz	8 oz
8 oz	8 oz	8 oz	8 oz	8 oz	8 oz	8 oz	8 oz

Hour Slept 1 2 3 4 5 6 7 8 9 10 11 12

Anxiety Level Today 1 2 3 4 5 6 7 8 9 10

Sadness Level Today 1 2 3 4 5 6 7 8 9 10

Cravings Level Today 1 2 3 4 5 6 7 8 9 10

Daily Reflection

Goal for today...

_____

_____

_____

I am proud of...

_____

_____

_____

I´m grateful for...

_____

_____

_____

Positive affirmation ...

_____

_____

_____

Days Sober ☐

Date :_____ S M T W R F S

Any Triggers today? Yes No

Appetite _____

Exercise today _____

Water Intake

8 oz	8 oz	8 oz	8 oz	8 oz	8 oz	8 oz	8 oz
8 oz	8 oz	8 oz	8 oz	8 oz	8 oz	8 oz	8 oz

Hour Slept 1 2 3 4 5 6 7 8 9 10 11 12

Anxiety Level Today 1 2 3 4 5 6 7 8 9 10

Sadness Level Today 1 2 3 4 5 6 7 8 9 10

Cravings Level Today 1 2 3 4 5 6 7 8 9 10

Daily Reflection

Goal for today...

_____

_____

_____

I am proud of...

_____

_____

_____

I'm grateful for...

_____

_____

_____

Positive affirmation ...

_____

_____

_____

Days Sober ☐

Date :_____ S M T W R F S

Any Triggers today? Yes No

Appetite _____

Exercise today _____

Water Intake

8 oz	8 oz	8 oz	8 oz	8 oz	8 oz	8 oz	8 oz
8 oz	8 oz	8 oz	8 oz	8 oz	8 oz	8 oz	8 oz

Hour Slept 1 2 3 4 5 6 7 8 9 10 11 12

Anxiety Level Today 1 2 3 4 5 6 7 8 9 10

Sadness Level Today 1 2 3 4 5 6 7 8 9 10

Cravings Level Today 1 2 3 4 5 6 7 8 9 10

Daily Reflection

Goal for today...

_____

_____

_____

I am proud of...

_____

_____

_____

I'm grateful for...

_____

_____

_____

Positive affirmation ...

_____

_____

_____

Days Sober ☐

Date : _____ S M T W R F S

Any Triggers today? Yes No

Appetite _____

Exercise today _____

Water Intake

8 oz	8 oz	8 oz	8 oz	8 oz	8 oz	8 oz	8 oz
8 oz	8 oz	8 oz	8 oz	8 oz	8 oz	8 oz	8 oz

Hour Slept 1 2 3 4 5 6 7 8 9 10 11 12

Anxiety Level Today 1 2 3 4 5 6 7 8 9 10

Sadness Level Today 1 2 3 4 5 6 7 8 9 10

Cravings Level Today 1 2 3 4 5 6 7 8 9 10

Daily Reflection

Goal for today...

_____

_____

_____

I am proud of...

_____

_____

_____

I´m grateful for...

_____

_____

_____

Positive affirmation ...

_____

_____

_____

Days Sober ☐

Date :_____ S M T W R F S

Any Triggers today? Yes No

Appetite _____

Exercise today _____

Water Intake | 8 oz | 8 oz | 8 oz | 8 oz | 8 oz | 8 oz | 8 oz | 8 oz |
| 8 oz | 8 oz | 8 oz | 8 oz | 8 oz | 8 oz | 8 oz | 8 oz |

Hour Slept 1 2 3 4 5 6 7 8 9 10 11 12

Anxiety Level Today 1 2 3 4 5 6 7 8 9 10

Sadness Level Today 1 2 3 4 5 6 7 8 9 10

Cravings Level Today 1 2 3 4 5 6 7 8 9 10

Daily Reflection

Goal for today...

_____

_____

_____

I am proud of...

_____

_____

_____

I'm grateful for...

_____

_____

_____

Positive affirmation ...

_____

_____

_____

Days Sober ☐

Date :_____ S M T W R F S

Any Triggers today? Yes No

Appetite _____

Exercise today _____

Water Intake

8 oz	8 oz	8 oz	8 oz	8 oz	8 oz	8 oz	8 oz
8 oz	8 oz	8 oz	8 oz	8 oz	8 oz	8 oz	8 oz

Hour Slept 1 2 3 4 5 6 7 8 9 10 11 12

Anxiety Level Today 1 2 3 4 5 6 7 8 9 10

Sadness Level Today 1 2 3 4 5 6 7 8 9 10

Cravings Level Today 1 2 3 4 5 6 7 8 9 10

Daily Reflection

Goal for today...
_____
_____
_____

I am proud of...
_____
_____
_____

I'm grateful for...
_____
_____
_____

Positive affirmation ...
_____
_____
_____

Days Sober ☐

Date :_____ S M T W R F S

Any Triggers today? Yes No

Appetite _____

Exercise today _____

Water Intake

8 oz	8 oz	8 oz	8 oz	8 oz	8 oz	8 oz	8 oz
8 oz	8 oz	8 oz	8 oz	8 oz	8 oz	8 oz	8 oz

Hour Slept 1 2 3 4 5 6 7 8 9 10 11 12

Anxiety Level Today 1 2 3 4 5 6 7 8 9 10

Sadness Level Today 1 2 3 4 5 6 7 8 9 10

Cravings Level Today 1 2 3 4 5 6 7 8 9 10

Daily Reflection

Goal for today...

_____

_____

_____

I am proud of...

_____

_____

_____

I'm grateful for...

_____

_____

_____

Positive affirmation ...

_____

_____

_____

Days Sober ☐

Date :_____ S M T W R F S

Any Triggers today? Yes No

Appetite _____

Exercise today _____

Water Intake

8 oz	8 oz	8 oz	8 oz	8 oz	8 oz	8 oz	8 oz
8 oz	8 oz	8 oz	8 oz	8 oz	8 oz	8 oz	8 oz

Hour Slept 1 2 3 4 5 6 7 8 9 10 11 12

Anxiety Level Today 1 2 3 4 5 6 7 8 9 10

Sadness Level Today 1 2 3 4 5 6 7 8 9 10

Cravings Level Today 1 2 3 4 5 6 7 8 9 10

Daily Reflection

Goal for today...

_____

_____

_____

I am proud of...

_____

_____

_____

I´m grateful for...

_____

_____

_____

Positive affirmation ...

_____

_____

_____

Days Sober ☐

Date :_____ S M T W R F S

Any Triggers today? Yes No

Appetite _____

Exercise today _____

Water Intake

8 oz	8 oz	8 oz	8 oz	8 oz	8 oz	8 oz	8 oz
8 oz	8 oz	8 oz	8 oz	8 oz	8 oz	8 oz	8 oz

Hour Slept 1 2 3 4 5 6 7 8 9 10 11 12

Anxiety Level Today 1 2 3 4 5 6 7 8 9 10

Sadness Level Today 1 2 3 4 5 6 7 8 9 10

Cravings Level Today 1 2 3 4 5 6 7 8 9 10

Daily Reflection

Goal for today...

_____

_____

_____

I am proud of...

_____

_____

_____

I´m grateful for...

_____

_____

_____

Positive affirmation ...

_____

_____

_____

Days Sober ☐

Date :_____ S M T W R F S

Any Triggers today? Yes No

Appetite _____

Exercise today _____

Water Intake | 8 oz | 8 oz | 8 oz | 8 oz | 8 oz | 8 oz | 8 oz | 8 oz |
| 8 oz | 8 oz | 8 oz | 8 oz | 8 oz | 8 oz | 8 oz | 8 oz |

Hour Slept 1 2 3 4 5 6 7 8 9 10 11 12

Anxiety Level Today 1 2 3 4 5 6 7 8 9 10

Sadness Level Today 1 2 3 4 5 6 7 8 9 10

Cravings Level Today 1 2 3 4 5 6 7 8 9 10

Daily Reflection

Goal for today...

_____

_____

_____

I am proud of...

_____

_____

_____

I'm grateful for...

_____

_____

_____

Positive affirmation ...

_____

_____

_____

Days Sober □

Date :_____ S M T W R F S

Any Triggers today? Yes No

Appetite _____

Exercise today _____

Water Intake | 8 oz | 8 oz | 8 oz | 8 oz | 8 oz | 8 oz | 8 oz | 8 oz |
| 8 oz | 8 oz | 8 oz | 8 oz | 8 oz | 8 oz | 8 oz | 8 oz |

Hour Slept 1 2 3 4 5 6 7 8 9 10 11 12

Anxiety Level Today 1 2 3 4 5 6 7 8 9 10

Sadness Level Today 1 2 3 4 5 6 7 8 9 10

Cravings Level Today 1 2 3 4 5 6 7 8 9 10

Daily Reflection

Goal for today...

_____

_____

_____

I am proud of...

_____

_____

_____

I'm grateful for...

_____

_____

_____

Positive affirmation ...

_____

_____

_____

Days Sober ☐

Date : _____ S M T W R F S

Any Triggers today? Yes No

Appetite _____

Exercise today _____

Water Intake

8 oz	8 oz	8 oz	8 oz	8 oz	8 oz	8 oz	8 oz
8 oz	8 oz	8 oz	8 oz	8 oz	8 oz	8 oz	8 oz

Hour Slept 1 2 3 4 5 6 7 8 9 10 11 12

Anxiety Level Today 1 2 3 4 5 6 7 8 9 10

Sadness Level Today 1 2 3 4 5 6 7 8 9 10

Cravings Level Today 1 2 3 4 5 6 7 8 9 10

Daily Reflection

Goal for today...
_____

_____

_____

I am proud of...
_____

_____

_____

I'm grateful for...
_____

_____

_____

Positive affirmation ...
_____

_____

_____

Days Sober ☐

Date :_____ S M T W R F S

Any Triggers today? Yes No

Appetite _____

Exercise today _____

Water Intake
8 oz	8 oz	8 oz	8 oz	8 oz	8 oz	8 oz	8 oz
8 oz	8 oz	8 oz	8 oz	8 oz	8 oz	8 oz	8 oz

Hour Slept 1 2 3 4 5 6 7 8 9 10 11 12

Anxiety Level Today 1 2 3 4 5 6 7 8 9 10

Sadness Level Today 1 2 3 4 5 6 7 8 9 10

Cravings Level Today 1 2 3 4 5 6 7 8 9 10

Daily Reflection

Goal for today...

_____

_____

_____

I am proud of...

_____

_____

_____

I´m grateful for...

_____

_____

_____

Positive affirmation ...

_____

_____

_____

Days Sober ☐

Date :_____ S M T W R F S

Any Triggers today? Yes No

Appetite _____

Exercise today _____

Water Intake | 8 oz | 8 oz | 8 oz | 8 oz | 8 oz | 8 oz | 8 oz | 8 oz |
| 8 oz | 8 oz | 8 oz | 8 oz | 8 oz | 8 oz | 8 oz | 8 oz |

Hour Slept 1 2 3 4 5 6 7 8 9 10 11 12

Anxiety Level Today 1 2 3 4 5 6 7 8 9 10

Sadness Level Today 1 2 3 4 5 6 7 8 9 10

Cravings Level Today 1 2 3 4 5 6 7 8 9 10

Daily Reflection

Goal for today...

_____

_____

_____

I am proud of...

_____

_____

_____

I'm grateful for...

_____

_____

_____

Positive affirmation ...

_____

_____

_____

Days Sober ☐

Date :_____ S M T W R F S

Any Triggers today? Yes No

Appetite _____

Exercise today _____

Water Intake

8 oz	8 oz	8 oz	8 oz	8 oz	8 oz	8 oz	8 oz
8 oz	8 oz	8 oz	8 oz	8 oz	8 oz	8 oz	8 oz

Hour Slept 1 2 3 4 5 6 7 8 9 10 11 12

Anxiety Level Today 1 2 3 4 5 6 7 8 9 10

Sadness Level Today 1 2 3 4 5 6 7 8 9 10

Cravings Level Today 1 2 3 4 5 6 7 8 9 10

Daily Reflection

Goal for today...

_____

_____

_____

I am proud of...

_____

_____

_____

I´m grateful for...

_____

_____

_____

Positive affirmation ...

_____

_____

_____

Days Sober ☐

Date :_____ S M T W R F S

Any Triggers today? Yes No

Appetite _____

Exercise today _____

Water Intake

8 oz	8 oz	8 oz	8 oz	8 oz	8 oz	8 oz	8 oz
8 oz	8 oz	8 oz	8 oz	8 oz	8 oz	8 oz	8 oz

Hour Slept 1 2 3 4 5 6 7 8 9 10 11 12

Anxiety Level Today 1 2 3 4 5 6 7 8 9 10

Sadness Level Today 1 2 3 4 5 6 7 8 9 10

Cravings Level Today 1 2 3 4 5 6 7 8 9 10

Daily Reflection

Goal for today...

_____

_____

_____

I am proud of...

_____

_____

_____

I'm grateful for...

_____

_____

_____

Positive affirmation ...

_____

_____

_____

Days Sober ☐

Date :_____ S M T W R F S

Any Triggers today? Yes No

Appetite _____

Exercise today _____

Water Intake

8 oz	8 oz	8 oz	8 oz	8 oz	8 oz	8 oz	8 oz
8 oz	8 oz	8 oz	8 oz	8 oz	8 oz	8 oz	8 oz

Hour Slept 1 2 3 4 5 6 7 8 9 10 11 12

Anxiety Level Today 1 2 3 4 5 6 7 8 9 10

Sadness Level Today 1 2 3 4 5 6 7 8 9 10

Cravings Level Today 1 2 3 4 5 6 7 8 9 10

Daily Reflection

Goal for today...

_____

_____

_____

I am proud of...

_____

_____

_____

I'm grateful for...

_____

_____

_____

Positive affirmation ...

_____

_____

_____

Days Sober ☐

Date : _____ S M T W R F S

Any Triggers today? Yes No

Appetite _____

Exercise today _____

Water Intake
8 oz	8 oz	8 oz	8 oz	8 oz	8 oz	8 oz	8 oz
8 oz	8 oz	8 oz	8 oz	8 oz	8 oz	8 oz	8 oz

Hour Slept 1 2 3 4 5 6 7 8 9 10 11 12

Anxiety Level Today 1 2 3 4 5 6 7 8 9 10

Sadness Level Today 1 2 3 4 5 6 7 8 9 10

Cravings Level Today 1 2 3 4 5 6 7 8 9 10

Daily Reflection

Goal for today...
_____

_____

_____

I am proud of...
_____

_____

_____

I'm grateful for...
_____

_____

_____

Positive affirmation ...
_____

_____

_____

Days Sober ☐

Date :_____ S M T W R F S

Any Triggers today? Yes No

Appetite _____

Exercise today _____

Water Intake

8 oz	8 oz	8 oz	8 oz	8 oz	8 oz	8 oz	8 oz
8 oz	8 oz	8 oz	8 oz	8 oz	8 oz	8 oz	8 oz

Hour Slept 1 2 3 4 5 6 7 8 9 10 11 12

Anxiety Level Today 1 2 3 4 5 6 7 8 9 10

Sadness Level Today 1 2 3 4 5 6 7 8 9 10

Cravings Level Today 1 2 3 4 5 6 7 8 9 10

Daily Reflection

Goal for today...

_____

_____

_____

I am proud of...

_____

_____

_____

I′m grateful for...

_____

_____

_____

Positive affirmation ...

_____

_____

_____

Days Sober ☐

Date : _____ S M T W R F S

Any Triggers today? Yes No

Appetite _____

Exercise today _____

Water Intake

8 oz	8 oz	8 oz	8 oz	8 oz	8 oz	8 oz	8 oz
8 oz	8 oz	8 oz	8 oz	8 oz	8 oz	8 oz	8 oz

Hour Slept 1 2 3 4 5 6 7 8 9 10 11 12

Anxiety Level Today 1 2 3 4 5 6 7 8 9 10

Sadness Level Today 1 2 3 4 5 6 7 8 9 10

Cravings Level Today 1 2 3 4 5 6 7 8 9 10

Daily Reflection

Goal for today...

_____

_____

_____

I am proud of...

_____

_____

_____

I´m grateful for...

_____

_____

_____

Positive affirmation ...

_____

_____

_____

Days Sober □

Date :_____ S M T W R F S

Any Triggers today? Yes No

Appetite _____

Exercise today _____

Water Intake | 8 oz | 8 oz | 8 oz | 8 oz | 8 oz | 8 oz | 8 oz | 8 oz |
| 8 oz | 8 oz | 8 oz | 8 oz | 8 oz | 8 oz | 8 oz | 8 oz |

Hour Slept 1 2 3 4 5 6 7 8 9 10 11 12

Anxiety Level Today 1 2 3 4 5 6 7 8 9 10

Sadness Level Today 1 2 3 4 5 6 7 8 9 10

Cravings Level Today 1 2 3 4 5 6 7 8 9 10

Daily Reflection

Goal for today...

_____

_____

_____

I am proud of...

_____

_____

_____

I'm grateful for...

_____

_____

_____

Positive affirmation ...

_____

_____

_____

Days Sober ☐

Date :_____ S M T W R F S

Any Triggers today? Yes No

Appetite _____

Exercise today _____

Water Intake

8 oz	8 oz	8 oz	8 oz	8 oz	8 oz	8 oz	8 oz
8 oz	8 oz	8 oz	8 oz	8 oz	8 oz	8 oz	8 oz

Hour Slept 1 2 3 4 5 6 7 8 9 10 11 12

Anxiety Level Today 1 2 3 4 5 6 7 8 9 10

Sadness Level Today 1 2 3 4 5 6 7 8 9 10

Cravings Level Today 1 2 3 4 5 6 7 8 9 10

Daily Reflection

Goal for today...

_____

_____

_____

I am proud of...

_____

_____

_____

I'm grateful for...

_____

_____

_____

Positive affirmation ...

_____

_____

_____

Days Sober ☐

Date :_____ S M T W R F S

Any Triggers today? Yes No

Appetite _____

Exercise today _____

Water Intake

8 oz	8 oz	8 oz	8 oz	8 oz	8 oz	8 oz	8 oz
8 oz	8 oz	8 oz	8 oz	8 oz	8 oz	8 oz	8 oz

Hour Slept 1 2 3 4 5 6 7 8 9 10 11 12

Anxiety Level Today 1 2 3 4 5 6 7 8 9 10

Sadness Level Today 1 2 3 4 5 6 7 8 9 10

Cravings Level Today 1 2 3 4 5 6 7 8 9 10

Daily Reflection

Goal for today...

_____

_____

_____

I am proud of...

_____

_____

_____

I ′ m grateful for...

_____

_____

_____

Positive affirmation ...

_____

_____

_____

Days Sober ☐

Date : _____ S M T W R F S

Any Triggers today? Yes No

Appetite _____

Exercise today _____

Water Intake

8 oz	8 oz	8 oz	8 oz	8 oz	8 oz	8 oz	8 oz
8 oz	8 oz	8 oz	8 oz	8 oz	8 oz	8 oz	8 oz

Hour Slept 1 2 3 4 5 6 7 8 9 10 11 12

Anxiety Level Today 1 2 3 4 5 6 7 8 9 10

Sadness Level Today 1 2 3 4 5 6 7 8 9 10

Cravings Level Today 1 2 3 4 5 6 7 8 9 10

Daily Reflection

Goal for today...

_____

_____

_____

I am proud of...

_____

_____

_____

I'm grateful for...

_____

_____

_____

Positive affirmation ...

_____

_____

_____

Days Sober ☐

Date :_____ S M T W R F S

Any Triggers today? Yes No

Appetite _____

Exercise today _____

Water Intake | 8 oz | 8 oz | 8 oz | 8 oz | 8 oz | 8 oz | 8 oz | 8 oz |
| 8 oz | 8 oz | 8 oz | 8 oz | 8 oz | 8 oz | 8 oz | 8 oz |

Hour Slept 1 2 3 4 5 6 7 8 9 10 11 12

Anxiety Level Today 1 2 3 4 5 6 7 8 9 10

Sadness Level Today 1 2 3 4 5 6 7 8 9 10

Cravings Level Today 1 2 3 4 5 6 7 8 9 10

Daily Reflection

Goal for today...

_____

_____

_____

I am proud of...

_____

_____

_____

I´m grateful for...

_____

_____

_____

Positive affirmation ...

_____

_____

_____

Days Sober ☐

Date : _____ S M T W R F S

Any Triggers today? Yes No

Appetite _____

Exercise today _____

Water Intake
8 oz	8 oz	8 oz	8 oz	8 oz	8 oz	8 oz	8 oz
8 oz	8 oz	8 oz	8 oz	8 oz	8 oz	8 oz	8 oz

Hour Slept 1 2 3 4 5 6 7 8 9 10 11 12

Anxiety Level Today 1 2 3 4 5 6 7 8 9 10

Sadness Level Today 1 2 3 4 5 6 7 8 9 10

Cravings Level Today 1 2 3 4 5 6 7 8 9 10

Daily Reflection

Goal for today...

_____

_____

_____

I am proud of...

_____

_____

_____

I'm grateful for...

_____

_____

_____

Positive affirmation ...

_____

_____

_____

Days Sober ☐

Date :_____ S M T W R F S

Any Triggers today? Yes No

Appetite _____

Exercise today _____

Water Intake | 8 oz | 8 oz | 8 oz | 8 oz | 8 oz | 8 oz | 8 oz | 8 oz |
| 8 oz | 8 oz | 8 oz | 8 oz | 8 oz | 8 oz | 8 oz | 8 oz |

Hour Slept 1 2 3 4 5 6 7 8 9 10 11 12

Anxiety Level Today 1 2 3 4 5 6 7 8 9 10

Sadness Level Today 1 2 3 4 5 6 7 8 9 10

Cravings Level Today 1 2 3 4 5 6 7 8 9 10

Daily Reflection

Goal for today...
_____
_____
_____

I am proud of...
_____
_____
_____

I'm grateful for...
_____
_____
_____

Positive affirmation ...
_____
_____
_____

Days Sober ☐

Date :_____ S M T W R F S

Any Triggers today? Yes No

Appetite _____

Exercise today _____

Water Intake | 8 oz | 8 oz | 8 oz | 8 oz | 8 oz | 8 oz | 8 oz | 8 oz |
| 8 oz | 8 oz | 8 oz | 8 oz | 8 oz | 8 oz | 8 oz | 8 oz |

Hour Slept 1 2 3 4 5 6 7 8 9 10 11 12

Anxiety Level Today 1 2 3 4 5 6 7 8 9 10

Sadness Level Today 1 2 3 4 5 6 7 8 9 10

Cravings Level Today 1 2 3 4 5 6 7 8 9 10

Daily Reflection

Goal for today...

_____

_____

_____

I am proud of...

_____

_____

_____

I'm grateful for...

_____

_____

_____

Positive affirmation ...

_____

_____

_____

Days Sober ☐

Date :_____ S M T W R F S

Any Triggers today? Yes No

Appetite _____

Exercise today _____

Water Intake

8 oz	8 oz	8 oz	8 oz	8 oz	8 oz	8 oz	8 oz
8 oz	8 oz	8 oz	8 oz	8 oz	8 oz	8 oz	8 oz

Hour Slept 1 2 3 4 5 6 7 8 9 10 11 12

Anxiety Level Today 1 2 3 4 5 6 7 8 9 10

Sadness Level Today 1 2 3 4 5 6 7 8 9 10

Cravings Level Today 1 2 3 4 5 6 7 8 9 10

Daily Reflection

Goal for today...

_____

_____

_____

I am proud of...

_____

_____

_____

I'm grateful for...

_____

_____

_____

Positive affirmation ...

_____

_____

_____

Days Sober ☐

Date :_____ S M T W R F S

Any Triggers today? Yes No

Appetite _____

Exercise today _____

Water Intake

8 oz	8 oz	8 oz	8 oz	8 oz	8 oz	8 oz	8 oz
8 oz	8 oz	8 oz	8 oz	8 oz	8 oz	8 oz	8 oz

Hour Slept 1 2 3 4 5 6 7 8 9 10 11 12

Anxiety Level Today 1 2 3 4 5 6 7 8 9 10

Sadness Level Today 1 2 3 4 5 6 7 8 9 10

Cravings Level Today 1 2 3 4 5 6 7 8 9 10

Daily Reflection

Goal for today...

_____

_____

_____

I am proud of...

_____

_____

_____

I'm grateful for...

_____

_____

_____

Positive affirmation ...

_____

_____

_____

Days Sober ☐

Date : _____ S M T W R F S

Any Triggers today? Yes No

Appetite _____

Exercise today _____

Water Intake

8 oz	8 oz	8 oz	8 oz	8 oz	8 oz	8 oz	8 oz
8 oz	8 oz	8 oz	8 oz	8 oz	8 oz	8 oz	8 oz

Hour Slept 1 2 3 4 5 6 7 8 9 10 11 12

Anxiety Level Today 1 2 3 4 5 6 7 8 9 10

Sadness Level Today 1 2 3 4 5 6 7 8 9 10

Cravings Level Today 1 2 3 4 5 6 7 8 9 10

Daily Reflection

Goal for today...

_____

_____

_____

I am proud of...

_____

_____

_____

I'm grateful for...

_____

_____

_____

Positive affirmation ...

_____

_____

_____

Days Sober ☐

Date : _____ S M T W R F S

Any Triggers today? Yes No

Appetite _____

Exercise today _____

Water Intake

8 oz	8 oz	8 oz	8 oz	8 oz	8 oz	8 oz	8 oz
8 oz	8 oz	8 oz	8 oz	8 oz	8 oz	8 oz	8 oz

Hour Slept 1 2 3 4 5 6 7 8 9 10 11 12

Anxiety Level Today 1 2 3 4 5 6 7 8 9 10

Sadness Level Today 1 2 3 4 5 6 7 8 9 10

Cravings Level Today 1 2 3 4 5 6 7 8 9 10

Daily Reflection

Goal for today...

_____

_____

_____

I am proud of...

_____

_____

_____

I´m grateful for...

_____

_____

_____

Positive affirmation ...

_____

_____

_____

Days Sober ☐

Date :＿＿＿＿＿＿ S M T W R F S

Any Triggers today? Yes No

Appetite ＿＿＿＿＿＿＿＿＿＿＿＿＿＿＿＿＿

Exercise today ＿＿＿＿＿＿＿＿＿＿＿＿＿＿

Water Intake

8 oz	8 oz	8 oz	8 oz	8 oz	8 oz	8 oz	8 oz
8 oz	8 oz	8 oz	8 oz	8 oz	8 oz	8 oz	8 oz

Hour Slept 1 2 3 4 5 6 7 8 9 10 11 12

Anxiety Level Today 1 2 3 4 5 6 7 8 9 10

Sadness Level Today 1 2 3 4 5 6 7 8 9 10

Cravings Level Today 1 2 3 4 5 6 7 8 9 10

Daily Reflection

Goal for today...

_____

_____

_____

I am proud of...

_____

_____

I'm grateful for...

_____

_____

Positive affirmation ...

_____

_____

_____

Days Sober ☐

Date : _____ S M T W R F S

Any Triggers today? Yes No

Appetite _____

Exercise today _____

Water Intake | 8 oz | 8 oz | 8 oz | 8 oz | 8 oz | 8 oz | 8 oz | 8 oz |
| 8 oz | 8 oz | 8 oz | 8 oz | 8 oz | 8 oz | 8 oz | 8 oz |

Hour Slept 1 2 3 4 5 6 7 8 9 10 11 12

Anxiety Level Today 1 2 3 4 5 6 7 8 9 10

Sadness Level Today 1 2 3 4 5 6 7 8 9 10

Cravings Level Today 1 2 3 4 5 6 7 8 9 10

Daily Reflection

Goal for today...

_____

_____

_____

I am proud of...

_____

_____

_____

I'm grateful for...

_____

_____

_____

Positive affirmation ...

_____

_____

_____

Days Sober ☐

Date :_____ S M T W R F S

Any Triggers today? Yes No

Appetite _____

Exercise today _____

Water Intake

8 oz	8 oz	8 oz	8 oz	8 oz	8 oz	8 oz	8 oz
8 oz	8 oz	8 oz	8 oz	8 oz	8 oz	8 oz	8 oz

Hour Slept 1 2 3 4 5 6 7 8 9 10 11 12

Anxiety Level Today 1 2 3 4 5 6 7 8 9 10

Sadness Level Today 1 2 3 4 5 6 7 8 9 10

Cravings Level Today 1 2 3 4 5 6 7 8 9 10

Daily Reflection

Goal for today...

_____

_____

_____

I am proud of...

_____

_____

_____

I'm grateful for...

_____

_____

_____

Positive affirmation ...

_____

_____

_____

Days Sober ☐

Date :_____ S M T W R F S

Any Triggers today? Yes No

Appetite _____

Exercise today _____

Water Intake

8 oz	8 oz	8 oz	8 oz	8 oz	8 oz	8 oz	8 oz
8 oz	8 oz	8 oz	8 oz	8 oz	8 oz	8 oz	8 oz

Hour Slept 1 2 3 4 5 6 7 8 9 10 11 12

Anxiety Level Today 1 2 3 4 5 6 7 8 9 10

Sadness Level Today 1 2 3 4 5 6 7 8 9 10

Cravings Level Today 1 2 3 4 5 6 7 8 9 10

Daily Reflection

Goal for today...

_____

_____

_____

I am proud of...

_____

_____

_____

I ' m grateful for...

_____

_____

_____

Positive affirmation ...

_____

_____

_____

Days Sober ☐

Date :_____ S M T W R F S

Any Triggers today? Yes No

Appetite _____

Exercise today _____

Water Intake

8 oz	8 oz	8 oz	8 oz	8 oz	8 oz	8 oz	8 oz
8 oz	8 oz	8 oz	8 oz	8 oz	8 oz	8 oz	8 oz

Hour Slept 1 2 3 4 5 6 7 8 9 10 11 12

Anxiety Level Today 1 2 3 4 5 6 7 8 9 10

Sadness Level Today 1 2 3 4 5 6 7 8 9 10

Cravings Level Today 1 2 3 4 5 6 7 8 9 10

Daily Reflection

Goal for today...

_____

_____

_____

I am proud of...

_____

_____

_____

I'm grateful for...

_____

_____

_____

Positive affirmation ...

_____

_____

_____

Days Sober □

Date :_____ S M T W R F S

Any Triggers today? Yes No

Appetite _____

Exercise today _____

Water Intake

8 oz	8 oz	8 oz	8 oz	8 oz	8 oz	8 oz	8 oz
8 oz	8 oz	8 oz	8 oz	8 oz	8 oz	8 oz	8 oz

Hour Slept 1 2 3 4 5 6 7 8 9 10 11 12

Anxiety Level Today 1 2 3 4 5 6 7 8 9 10

Sadness Level Today 1 2 3 4 5 6 7 8 9 10

Cravings Level Today 1 2 3 4 5 6 7 8 9 10

Daily Reflection

Goal for today...

_____

_____

_____

I am proud of...

_____

_____

_____

I'm grateful for...

_____

_____

_____

Positive affirmation ...

_____

_____

_____

Days Sober ☐

Date :_____ S M T W R F S

Any Triggers today? Yes No

Appetite _____

Exercise today _____

Water Intake | 8 OZ | 8 OZ | 8 OZ | 8 OZ | 8 OZ | 8 OZ | 8 OZ | 8 OZ |
| 8 OZ | 8 OZ | 8 OZ | 8 OZ | 8 OZ | 8 OZ | 8 OZ | 8 OZ |

Hour Slept 1 2 3 4 5 6 7 8 9 10 11 12

Anxiety Level Today 1 2 3 4 5 6 7 8 9 10

Sadness Level Today 1 2 3 4 5 6 7 8 9 10

Cravings Level Today 1 2 3 4 5 6 7 8 9 10

Daily Reflection

Goal for today...

_____

_____

_____

I am proud of...

_____

_____

_____

I'm grateful for...

_____

_____

_____

Positive affirmation ...

_____

_____

_____

Days Sober ☐

Date :_____ S M T W R F S

Any Triggers today? Yes No

Appetite _____

Exercise today _____

Water Intake

8 oz	8 oz	8 oz	8 oz	8 oz	8 oz	8 oz	8 oz
8 oz	8 oz	8 oz	8 oz	8 oz	8 oz	8 oz	8 oz

Hour Slept 1 2 3 4 5 6 7 8 9 10 11 12

Anxiety Level Today 1 2 3 4 5 6 7 8 9 10

Sadness Level Today 1 2 3 4 5 6 7 8 9 10

Cravings Level Today 1 2 3 4 5 6 7 8 9 10

Daily Reflection

Goal for today...

_____

_____

_____

I am proud of...

_____

_____

_____

I'm grateful for...

_____

_____

_____

Positive affirmation ...

_____

_____

_____

Days Sober ☐

Date :_____ S M T W R F S

Any Triggers today? Yes No

Appetite _____

Exercise today _____

Water Intake

8 oz	8 oz	8 oz	8 oz	8 oz	8 oz	8 oz	8 oz
8 oz	8 oz	8 oz	8 oz	8 oz	8 oz	8 oz	8 oz

Hour Slept 1 2 3 4 5 6 7 8 9 10 11 12

Anxiety Level Today 1 2 3 4 5 6 7 8 9 10

Sadness Level Today 1 2 3 4 5 6 7 8 9 10

Cravings Level Today 1 2 3 4 5 6 7 8 9 10

Daily Reflection

Goal for today...

_____

_____

_____

I am proud of...

_____

_____

_____

I'm grateful for...

_____

_____

_____

Positive affirmation ...

_____

_____

_____

Days Sober ☐

Date :_____ S M T W R F S

Any Triggers today? Yes No

Appetite _____

Exercise today _____

Water Intake

8 oz	8 oz	8 oz	8 oz	8 oz	8 oz	8 oz	8 oz
8 oz	8 oz	8 oz	8 oz	8 oz	8 oz	8 oz	8 oz

Hour Slept 1 2 3 4 5 6 7 8 9 10 11 12

Anxiety Level Today 1 2 3 4 5 6 7 8 9 10

Sadness Level Today 1 2 3 4 5 6 7 8 9 10

Cravings Level Today 1 2 3 4 5 6 7 8 9 10

Daily Reflection

Goal for today...
_____

_____

_____

I am proud of...
_____

_____

_____

I´m grateful for...
_____

_____

_____

Positive affirmation ...
_____

_____

_____

Days Sober ☐

Date :_____ S M T W R F S

Any Triggers today? Yes No

Appetite _____

Exercise today _____

Water Intake

8 oz	8 oz	8 oz	8 oz	8 oz	8 oz	8 oz	8 oz
8 oz	8 oz	8 oz	8 oz	8 oz	8 oz	8 oz	8 oz

Hour Slept 1 2 3 4 5 6 7 8 9 10 11 12

Anxiety Level Today 1 2 3 4 5 6 7 8 9 10

Sadness Level Today 1 2 3 4 5 6 7 8 9 10

Cravings Level Today 1 2 3 4 5 6 7 8 9 10

Daily Reflection

Goal for today...

_____

_____

I am proud of...

_____

_____

I'm grateful for...

_____

_____

Positive affirmation ...

_____

_____

Days Sober ☐

Date :_____ S M T W R F S

Any Triggers today? Yes No

Appetite _____

Exercise today _____

Water Intake | 8 oz | 8 oz | 8 oz | 8 oz | 8 oz | 8 oz | 8 oz | 8 oz |
| 8 oz | 8 oz | 8 oz | 8 oz | 8 oz | 8 oz | 8 oz | 8 oz |

Hour Slept 1 2 3 4 5 6 7 8 9 10 11 12

Anxiety Level Today 1 2 3 4 5 6 7 8 9 10

Sadness Level Today 1 2 3 4 5 6 7 8 9 10

Cravings Level Today 1 2 3 4 5 6 7 8 9 10

Daily Reflection

Goal for today...

_____

_____

_____

I am proud of...

_____

_____

I'm grateful for...

_____

_____

Positive affirmation ...

_____

_____

_____

Days Sober ☐

Date : _____ S M T W R F S

Any Triggers today? Yes No

Appetite _____

Exercise today _____

Water Intake

8 oz	8 oz	8 oz	8 oz	8 oz	8 oz	8 oz	8 oz
8 oz	8 oz	8 oz	8 oz	8 oz	8 oz	8 oz	8 oz

Hour Slept 1 2 3 4 5 6 7 8 9 10 11 12

Anxiety Level Today 1 2 3 4 5 6 7 8 9 10

Sadness Level Today 1 2 3 4 5 6 7 8 9 10

Cravings Level Today 1 2 3 4 5 6 7 8 9 10

Daily Reflection

Goal for today...

_____

_____

_____

I am proud of...

_____

_____

_____

I´m grateful for...

_____

_____

_____

Positive affirmation ...

_____

_____

_____

Days Sober ☐

Date :_____ S M T W R F S

Any Triggers today? Yes No

Appetite _____

Exercise today _____

Water Intake

8 oz	8 oz	8 oz	8 oz	8 oz	8 oz	8 oz	8 oz
8 oz	8 oz	8 oz	8 oz	8 oz	8 oz	8 oz	8 oz

Hour Slept 1 2 3 4 5 6 7 8 9 10 11 12

Anxiety Level Today 1 2 3 4 5 6 7 8 9 10

Sadness Level Today 1 2 3 4 5 6 7 8 9 10

Cravings Level Today 1 2 3 4 5 6 7 8 9 10

Daily Reflection

Goal for today...
_____
_____
_____

I am proud of...
_____
_____
_____

I´m grateful for...
_____
_____
_____

Positive affirmation ...
_____
_____
_____

Days Sober ☐

Date : _____ S M T W R F S

Any Triggers today? Yes No

Appetite _____

Exercise today _____

Water Intake

8 oz	8 oz	8 oz	8 oz	8 oz	8 oz	8 oz	8 oz
8 oz	8 oz	8 oz	8 oz	8 oz	8 oz	8 oz	8 oz

Hour Slept 1 2 3 4 5 6 7 8 9 10 11 12

Anxiety Level Today 1 2 3 4 5 6 7 8 9 10

Sadness Level Today 1 2 3 4 5 6 7 8 9 10

Cravings Level Today 1 2 3 4 5 6 7 8 9 10

Daily Reflection

Goal for today...

_____

_____

_____

I am proud of...

_____

_____

_____

I′m grateful for...

_____

_____

_____

Positive affirmation ...

_____

_____

_____

If you found this
recovery journal
helpful,
check out all that

RECOVERY

PRESS

has to offer
on Amazon

Made in the USA
Las Vegas, NV
12 June 2024

91018284R00077